A City Lullaby

by

Katy Brodski-Quigley

**For my grandmother, the city girl,
And all the children of the cities.**

Cities never-ever sleep,
But live creatures do.

Red-tailed hawk sleeps in the nest,

Tigers in the zoo.

Sparrows on the lamp,

Froggie dreams in cozy tank
Where it's nice and damp.

Pigeons on the wire
Dream of cheerios and bread
That their hearts desire.

On the crossroads down below
"Whoosh" - the cars go by.

Over parks
where tall trees grow
Blinking airplanes fly.

Headlights streak
     and street lights glow,
Windows squares of color throw,

Mommies curtains gently draw
    And to sleep we go.